AS IF

AS IF

Poems New and Selected

John Ciardi

RUTGERS UNIVERSITY PRESS

New Brunswick, New Jersey, 1955

To Constance Caraway
with all our love for all her shining

Contents

TO JUDITH   1

WAR POEMS   11

    The Health of Captains   13
    Poem for My Twenty-Ninth Birthday   14
    Elegy   17
    Elegy Just in Case   18
    Sea Burial   21
    V-J Day   22
    On a Photo of Sgt. Ciardi a Year Later   23
    Two Songs for a Gunner   24

TRIBAL POEMS   25

    The Lamb   27
    The Evil Eye   29
    My Father's Watch   30
    Mystic River   32
    Elegy   34
    Home Revisited: Midnight   37
    Days   39
    Elegy for Sandro   41
    Thursday   43
    A Variation on Some Lines   50
    Survival in Missouri   51
    To My Father   52

Three Views of a Mother   55
Poem for My Thirty-Ninth Birthday   59

POEMS LOOKING OUT   63

Doctor Faustus   65
Child Horvald to the Dark Tower Came   68
A Box Comes Home   70
Newsreel   71
At a Concert of Music, Remembering the
    Dead in Korea   72
A Thought About Shiek Bedreddin   74
The Convert   75
In the Witch-Hunting Season   77
Kristóffer Second   78
Elegy for G. B. Shaw   80
The Invasion of Sleep Walkers   82
I Thanked the Lunatic for a Particular View   83
Lines for Woodlawn   84

PRAYERS   85

Temptation   87
Flowering Quince   88
Sunday Morning   90
Measurements   94
Annals   95
Fragment of a Bas Relief   96
Carlo Crivelli Muses Before a Madonna   97
Two Egrets   103

POEMS LOOKING IN   105

  On the Birth of Jeffrey to William and Bar-
    bara Harding   107
  Laing's Goat   109
  The Size of a Universe   110
  Thoughts on Looking into a Thicket   112
  A Sermon Beginning with the Portrait of a
    Man   114

SOME SCENES   115

  On Looking East to the Sea with a Sunset
    Behind Me   117
  Landscapes of My Name   120
  Chorus   121
  A Visit to Aunt Francesca   122
  March Morning   123
  Gulls from a Fantail   124
  The Cow   127
  Elegy for Jog   128
  Domesticity   128
  Lines While Walking Home from a Party on
    Charles Street   129
  Cezannc   130
  A Shore, Half in a Dream   131

FRAGMENTS FROM ITALY   133

TO JUDITH

i

Men marry what they need. I marry you,
morning by morning, day by day, night by night,
and every marriage makes this marriage new.

In the broken name of heaven, in the light
that shatters granite, by the spitting shore,
in air that leaps and wobbles like a kite,

I marry you from time and a great door
is shut and stays shut against wind, sea, stone,
sunburst, and heavenfall. And home once more

inside our walls of skin and struts of bone,
man-woman, woman-man, and each the other,
I marry you by all dark and all dawn

and have my laugh at death. Why should I bother
the flies about me? Let them buzz and do.
Men marry their queen, their daughter, or their mother

by hidden names, but that thin buzz whines through:
where reasons are no reason, cause is true.
Men marry what they need. I marry you.

ii

My dear, darkened in sleep, turned from the moon
That riots on curtain-stir with every breeze
Leaping in moths of light across your back . . .
Far off, then soft and sudden as petals shower
Down from wired roses—silently, all at once—
You turn, abandoned and naked, all let down
In ferny streams of sleep and petaled thighs
Rippling into my flesh's buzzing garden.

Far and familiar your body's myth map lights,
Traveled by moon and dapple. Sagas were curved
Like scimitars to your hips. The raiders' ships
All sailed to your one port. And watchfires burned
Your image on the hills. Sweetly you drown
Male centuries in your chiaroscuro tide
Of breast and breath. And all my memory's shores
You frighten perfectly, washed familiar and far.

Ritual wars have climbed your shadowed flank
Where bravos dreaming of fair women tore
Rock out of rock to have your cities down
In loot of hearths and trophies of desire.
And desert monks have fought your image back
In a hysteria of mad skeletons.
Bravo and monk (the heads and tails of love)
I stand, a spinning coin of wish and dread,

Counting our life, our chairs, our books and walls,
Our clock whose radium eye and insect voice
Owns all our light and shade, and your white shell
Spiraled in moonlight on the bed's white beach;
Thinking, I might press you to my ear
And all your coils fall out in sounds of surf
Washing a mystery sudden as you are
A light on light in light beyond the light.

Child, child, and making legend of my wish
Fastened alive into your naked sprawl —
Stir once to stop my fear and miser's panic
That time shall have you last and legendry
Undress to old bones from its moon brocade.
Yet sleep and keep our prime of time alive
Before that death of legend. My dear of all

Saga and century, sleep in familiar-far.
Time still must tick *this is, I am, we are.*

iii

Sometimes the foundering fury that directs
the prayer through storm, the sucking mouth;
sometimes a gentleness like a parent sex,
sometimes an aimless tasting mild as broth

or the drugged eye of the invalid, sometimes
the naked arm laid loose along the grass
to the brown-eyed breast and the great terms
of the turning flank printed by root and moss.

Sometimes a country in a white bird's eye
coasting the shells of cities in their past,
the roads that stretch to nothing but away,
a horseman wandering in his own dust—

say you were beautiful those years ago,
flush as the honey-blonde who rode the shell
in Sandro Botticelli's studio,
and what we are now, we were then,

and lost, and found again—what shall we wish
to visit from ourselves against that death
but their imagination on our flesh?
There is no other body in all myth.

iv

I look through my dead friend's eyes at the house of love:
plaster scabs from lath, windows break out
in toothy gapes, doors stagger from their pins.
See what a feast this is, my love, my love,
our shelves of mouse turds, dusts, and dirty damps!

I try this vision on like the wrong glasses
and every straightness quivers to a blur,
and every surface whorls to drink me in.
Well then, this is a world for twisted eyes.
Or if my eye offend me I'll pluck it out.

And still be chanceled in our breathing bed,
the dusk behind the taper and the cup,
as I was once—a holy man, though I lost
my holy ghost, my terror, and my sin
when I had got my own death down by heart.

And there's no nonsense like it. If I forgive
that death, I lose my last prayer. Let us live.

V

The deaths about you when you stir in sleep
hasten me toward you. Out of the bitter mouth
that sours the dark, I sigh for what we are
who heave our vines of blood against the air.

Old men have touched their dreaming to their hearts:
that is their age. I touch the moment's dream
and shrink like them into the thing we are
who drag our sleeps behind us like a fear.

Murderers have prayed their victims to escape,
then killed because they stayed. In murdering time
I think of rescues from the thing we are
who cannot slip one midnight from the year.

Scholars have sunk their eyes in penitence
for sins themselves invented. Sick as Faust
I trade with devils, damning what we are
who walk our dreams out on a leaning tower.

Saints on their swollen knees have banged at death:
it opened; they fell still. I bang at life
to knock the walls away from what we are
who raise our deaths about us when we stir.

Lovers unfevering sonnets from their blood
have burned with patience, laboring to make fast
one blood-beat of the bursting thing we are.
I have no time. I love you by despair.

8

Till on the midnight of the thing we are
the deaths that nod about us when we stir,
wake and become. Once past that fitful hour
our best will be to dream of what we were.

WAR POEMS

The Health of Captains

All wars are boyish and are fought by boys.
                                        —Melville

The health of captains is the sex of war:
the pump of sperm built in their polished thighs
powers all their blood; the dead, like paid-off whores,
sleep through the mornings where the captains rise.

The gloss of captains is the flags of war:
the polished shoes of death, the brass of poise,
the profile fitted like a tool in leather
between the paddlewheels of marching boys.

The deaths of captains are the tic of war:
the bone-hinged jaw punched open by surprise
under the marshsmoke- and cycloning-air
whose devils suck the last light from their eyes.

Fife and drum dollops drop to bins of grass
the health and gloss and deaths the captains are.
The boys behind the dead boys change their brass.
The womb of woman is the kit of war.

Poem for My Twenty-Ninth Birthday

Once more the pre-dawn throbs on engine sound
Down coral slope, papaya grove, and pine,
Into the sea whose pastures girdle round
The native in his jungle, I in mine,
And you in yours, O gentle stay at home:
Your talons, too, have raked the living bone.

We waken, and the cities of our day
Move down a cross-haired bombsight in the mind.
The thoughtless led, those only in the way,
The powerful by intent, wake there and find
Their jungles closing, each man tangled tight
Into this day that may not last till night.

Now I have named another year of time
Learning to count not mine but a world's age.
And on the morning of no birth I climb
To sign in fire our sullen heritage:
The bomb whose metal carcass, dressed and bled,
Is our day's gift to populate the dead.

See by his steaming garden in the dawn
The native change his waiting as we pass
His centuries upon this flowering stone.
Our trucks, arrived in clouds of dust and gas,
Coat his green jungle till the daily rain.
He sees us past and turns to wait again.

His is the simplest darkness; our grotesque
Of straps and buckles, parachutes and guns,

Our gear of kit and cartridge, helmet, mask,
Life vest, rations, and the elegance
Of all our conscious gestures and our gum,
Darken us further than his guess can come.

We leave his green past. On a metal din
Our gears resolve us from the valley night
To plateaus where the rapt emblazoned fin
Our perfect bomber lifts to the first light
Mounts on the air up which the morning sun
Prophesies Asia and a death to come.

Already now, my dear, this turning sun
Has been your day, and here returns to me
Where I inherit on a bomber's run
Your image from the sundial of the sea.
I dream you smiling, waking fleshed in grace,
And see, a gunsight photographs your face.

I cannot lose my darkness. Posed and dressed,
I touch the metal womb our day will ride.
We take our places while a switch is pressed,
And sun and engines rise from the hillside—
A single motion and a single fire
To burn, return, and live upon desire.

Look at the sea and learn how malice shines
Bright as a noon come down through colored glass.
We arc the soaring madness of our times
Marking our own flown never-ending loss.

The whitecaps strewn like lint on a stone floor
Wait, will swallow, close, and wait once more.

Now, westering, our day has named its course:
Far down in frost and tiny symmetry
Fuji, the magic mountain of what was,
Places our past on the trajectory
Of the co-sined and wind-computed fall
Our bombs descend to save or kill us all.

And last, by dark, we have our rock again:
Our wheels touch and our waiting lives return.
Far off the dead are lying in the rain,
And on their dark the ruined cities burn
Our jungles down with light enough to see
The last compassionate necessity.

Elegy

For Kurt Porjescz, Missing in Action, 1 April 1945

Some gone like boys to school wearing their badges,
Some calmly with a look of measuring,
While every wind is April in the hedges
On a grotesque of bony birds who sing
A metal note, weathering and weathering.

Here in this good green scene above the sea
The April world astonishes my look.
This island rock in space turns flowering endlessly
To peaks of cloud still mounting where you took
Your last high passage and your broken luck.

The boys are flowers: they strew themselves in seed
And spring again, anonymous and pure,
For the same eye to follow the same deed
Of bending in the wind, and soon and sure
Fade, fold, and fall out of the sunburst hour.

Clouds had them once, and wreckage mars them now.
And the same wreckage scatters on your fall.
Spring, which amazes more than we allow
Of our dark selves to show, sets equally after all
On the blind wreck of gland and rationale.

Now only memory keeps its aftermotion.
Good-bye, where no luck serves, nor any word,
Across a swell of sky and cloudy ocean
While April wind and bony bird
Discuss our futures, and have not concurred.

Elegy Just in Case

Here lie Ciardi's pearly bones
In their ripe organic mess.
Jungle blown, his chromosomes
Breed to a new address.

Progenies of orchids seek
The fracture's white spilled lymph.
And his heart's red valve will leak
Fountains for a protein nymph.

Was it bullets or a wind
Or a rip-cord fouled on Chance?
Artifacts the natives find
Decorate them when they dance.

Here lies the sgt.'s mortal wreck
Lily spiked and termite kissed,
Spiders pendant from his neck
And a beetle on his wrist.

Bring the tic and southern flies
Where the land crabs run unmourning
Through a night of jungle skies
To a climeless morning.

And bring the chalked eraser here
Fresh from rubbing out his name.
Burn the crew-board for a bier.
(Also Colonel what's-his-name.)

Let no dice be stored and still.
Let no poker deck be torn.
But pour the smuggled rye until
The barracks threshold is outworn.

File the papers, pack the clothes,
Send the coded word through air—
"We regret and no one knows
Where the sgt. goes from here."

"Missing as of inst. oblige,
Deepest sorrow and remain—"
Shall I grin at persiflage?
Could I have my skin again

Would I choose a business form
Stilted mute as a giraffe,
Or a pinstripe unicorn
On a cashier's epitaph?

Darling, darling, just in case
Rivets fail or engines burn,
I forget the time and place
But your flesh was sweet to learn.

In the grammar of not yet
Let me name one verb for chance,
Scholarly to one regret:
That I leave your mood and tense.

Swift and single as a shark
I have seen you churn my sleep;
Now if beetles hunt my dark
What will beetles find to keep?

Fractured meat and open bone—
Nothing single or surprised.
Fragments of a written stone,
Undeciphered but surmised.

Through the sea's crust of prisms looking up
Into the run of light above the swell,
And down a fathom, down a fathom more
Into the darkness closing like a shell.

Oblique, like fall of leaves down the wet glide
Of season and surrender from the tree
Of life across the windows of a wind
To the final ruined lawn beneath a sea —

Glide, glide and fall. How lightly death goes down
Into the crushing fog, pale and refracted.
Seen dimly and then lost, like jellyfish
Flowering a tide, expanded, then contracted,

Once more expanded, and then closed forever
To make a stain on stone and liquefy
The memory that kissed a mountain girl
And ran on grass as if it could not die.

V-J Day

On the tallest day in time the dead came back.
Clouds met us in the pastures past a world.
By short wave the releases of a rack
Exploded on the interphone's new word.

Halfway past Iwo we jettisoned to sea
Ten tons of arrows from the Eagle's claws.
They fell and followed. Half nostalgically
We watched them spout a fountain from the troughs.

Lightened, we banked like jays, antennae squawking.
The four wild metal halos of our props
Blurred into time. The interphone was talking
Abracadabra to the cumulus tops:

Dreamboat three-one to Yearsend—loud and clear,
Angels one-two, on course at one-six-nine.
Magellan to Balboa. Propwash to Century.
How do you read me? Bombay to Valentine.

Fading and out. And all the dead were homing.
(*Wisecrack to Halfmast. Doom to Memory.*)
On the tallest day in time we saw them coming,
Wheels jammed, and flaming, on a metal sea.

On a Photo of Sgt. Ciardi a Year Later

The sgt. stands so fluently in leather,
So poster-holstered and so newsreel-jawed
As death's costumed and fashionable brother,
My civil memory is overawed.

Behind him see the circuses of doom
Dance a finale chorus on the sun.
He leans on gunsights, doesn't give a damn
For dice or stripes, and waits to see the fun.

The cameraman whose ornate public eye
Invented that fine bravura look of calm
At murderous clocks hung ticking in the sky
Palmed the deception off without a qualm.

Even the camera, focused and exact
To a two dimensional conclusion,
Uttered its formula of physical fact
Only to lend data to illusion.

The camera always lies. By a law of perception
The obvious surface is always an optical ruse.
The leather was living tissue in its own dimension,
The holsters held benzedrine tablets, the guns were no use.

The careful slouch and dangling cigarette
Were always superstitious as Amen.
The shadow under the shadow is never caught:
The camera photographs the cameraman.

Two Songs for a Gunner

i

Firing Tracers
When I was dangerous tracers leaped from me.
What a wild fountain I sprayed at the zodiac
Falling how-many-colored to sea-dark
Of the world's body under, where powerfully
I rode it and rode it done. "Look, Mother, how gay
And luminous a sperm I spend in play!"

ii

Being Fired At
When I was danger's the tracers' endless
Jeweled cobra struck at my running tomb
In a cloud. How chaste and sweet a womb
I cowered in to praise its luminous
Waver and fall from power. And as it fell,
How deep an egg I curled in very well.

TRIBAL POEMS

A month before Easter
Came the time of the lamb
Staked on my lawn
To frisk and feed and be
My tenderest playmate,
Sweeter for being
Sudden and perilous.

Fed from my hand,
Brushed by my love,
An acrid and tangled wool
Grew clumsy and cardinal.
The lamb is a beast of knees.
A thin and tipsy chant
Quavers in it.

Year by year the lamb
Danced the black lenten season.
On the Thursday of sorrow
It disappeared.
On the Friday of blood I knew
What business was in the cellar
And wept a little.

But ah came Easter
My lamb, my sufferer, rose,
Rose from the charnel cellar,
Glowed golden brown
On religious plenty.
How gravely he was broken,
Sprigged for a bridal.

I praise the soil
In the knuckle and habit
Of my feeding parents
Who knew anciently
How the holy and edible
Are one, are life, must be loved
And surrendered.

My tears for the lamb
Were the bath it sprang from
Washed and risen
To its own demand
For a defenseless death.
After the lamb had been wept for
Its flesh was Easter.

The Evil Eye

(The belief in the Evil Eye is a still-surviving superstition among Italian peasants. One method of detecting its presence is to pour olive oil on a saucer of holy water. The shapes assumed by the oil can then be read by the gifted.)

Nona poured oil on the water and saw the eye
　　Form on my birth. Zia beat me with bay,
　　Fennel, and barley to scourge the devil away.
I doubt I needed so much excuse to cry.

From Sister Maria Immaculata there came
　　A crucifix, a vow of nine days' prayer,
　　And a scapular stitched with virgin's hair.
The eye glowed on the water all the same.

By Felice, the midwife, I was hung with a tin
　　Fish stuffed with garlic and bread crumbs.
　　Three holy waters washed the breast for my gums.
Still the eye glared, wide as original sin,

On the deepest pools of women midnight-spoken
　　To ward my clamoring soul from the clutch of hell,
　　Lest growing I be no comfort and dying swell
More than a grave with horror. Still unbroken

The eye glared through the roosts of all their clucking.
　　"Jesu," cried Mother, "why is he deviled so?"
　　"Baptism without delay," said Father Cosmo.
"This one is not for sprinkling but for ducking."

So in came meat and wine and the feast was on.
    I wore a palm frond in my lace, and sewn
    To my swaddling band a hoop and three beads of bone
For the Trinity. And they ducked me and called me John.

And ate the meat and drank the wine, and the eye
    Closed on the water. All this fell between
    My first scream and first name in 1916,
The year of the war and the influenza, when I

Was not yet ready for evil or my own name,
Though I had one already and the other came.

My Father's Watch

One night I dreamed I was locked in my Father's watch
With Ptolemy and twenty-one ruby stars
Mounted on spheres and the Primum Mobile
Coiled and gleaming to the end of space
And the notched spheres eating each other's rinds
To the last tooth of time, and the case closed.

What dawns and sunsets clattered from the conveyer
Over my head and his while the ruby stars
Whirled rosettes about their golden poles.
"Man, what a show!" I cried. "Infinite order!"
Ptolemy sang. "The miracle of things
Wound endlessly to the first energy
From which all matter quickened and took place!"

"What makes it shine so bright?" I leaned across
Fast between two teeth and touched the mainspring.
At once all hell broke loose. Over our heads
Squadrons of band saws ripped at one another
And broken teeth spewed meteors of flak
From the red stars.

                    You couldn't dream that din:
I broke and ran past something into somewhere
Beyond a glimpse of Ptolemy split open,
And woke on a numbered dial where two black swords
Spun under a crystal dome. There, looking up
In one flash as the two swords closed and came,
I saw my Father's face frown through the glass.

Mystic River

i

The dirty river by religious explorers
Named Mysticke and recorded forever into its future
Civilization of silt and sewerage, recovers
The first sweet moon of time tonight. A tremor
More thought than breeze, more exhalation than motion
Stirs the gold water totem, Snake of the Moon.

"A most pleasynge gentle and salubrious river
Wherein lieth no hindraunce of rock nor shoal
To the distresse of nauvigation, but ever
Aboundaunce of landynge and of fisherie, and withal
Distillynge so sweet an air thorough its course
Sith it runneth salt from the sea, fresh from the source

"And altereth daily through its greater length
Thus chaungynge and refreshynge the valleys breath,
That," wrote the Gods, "God grauntynge strength
We took up laundes, and here untill oure death
Shall be oure hearthes oure labour and oure joye."
But what the Gods will have they first destroy.

Still Mystic lights the wake of Gods—the moon
Dances on pollution, the fish are fled
Into a finer instinct of revulsion
Than Gods had. And the Gods are dead,
Their sloops and river rotted, and their bones
That scrubbed old conscience down like holystones

Powdered imperceptibly. Their land
Is an old land where nothing's planted
Beside the rollerdrome and hot dog stand —
Still Mystic lights the wake of Gods, still haunted
By the reversing moon. "Let me be clean,"
It cries and cries, but there are years between.

ii

And I have stoned and swum and sculled them all:
Naked behind the birches at the cove
Where Winthrop built a landing and a yawl
And tabloids found a famous corpse of love
Hacked small and parceled into butcher's paper,
Joe La Conti stumbled on an old pauper

Dying of epilepsy or DT's,
And I came running naked to watch the fit.
We had to dress to run for the police.
But did we run for help or the joy of it?
And who was dying at the sight of blood?
Weeks long we conjured its traces in the mud

And there was no trace. Later above the cat-tails
A house frame grew, and another, and then another.
Our naked bank bled broken tiles and nails.
We made a raft and watched the alewife smother.
But there our play drank fever, and Willie Crosby
Went home from that dirty water and stayed to die.

iii

So I know death is a dirty river
At the edge of history, through the middle of towns,
At the backs of stores, and under the cantilever
Stations of bridges where the moon drowns
Pollution in its own illusion of light.
Oh rotten time, rot from my mind tonight!

Let me be lit to the bone in this one stir,
And where the Gods grew rich and positive
From their ruinous landing, I'll attend disaster
Like night birds over a wake, dark and alive
Above the shuttered house, and, bound and free,
Wheel on the wing, find food in flight, and be

Captured by light, drawn down and down and down
By moonshine, streetlamps, windows, moving rays.
By all that shines in all the caved-in town
Where Mystic in the crazy moon outstays
The death of Gods, and makes a life of light
That breaks, but calls a million birds to flight.

My father was born with a spade in his hand and traded it
for a needle's eye to sit his days cross-legged on tables
till he could sit no more, then sold insurance, reading
the ten-cent-a-week lives like logarithms from
the Tables of Metropolitan to their prepaid tombstones.

Years of the little dimes twinkling on kitchen tables
at Mrs. Fauci's at Mrs. Locatelli's at Mrs. Cataldo's
(*Arrividerla, signora. A la settimana prossima. Mi saluta,
la prego, il marito. Ciao, Anna. Bye-bye.*)
—known as a Debit. And with his ten-year button

he opened a long dream like a piggy bank, spilling the dimes
like mountain water into the moss of himself, and bought
ten piney lots in Wilmington. Sunday by Sunday
he took the train to his woods and walked under the trees
to leave his print on his own land, a patron of seasons.

I have done nothing as perfect as my father's Sundays
on his useless lots. Gardens he dreamed from briar tangle
and the swampy back slope of his ridge rose over him
more flowering than Brazil. Maples transformed to figs,
and briar to blood-blue grapes in his look around

when he sat on a stone with his wine-jug and cheese beside
   him,
his collar and coat on a branch, his shirt open,
his derby back on his head like a standing turtle. A big
man he was. When he sang *Celeste Aida* the woods
filled as if a breeze were swelling through them.

When he stopped, I thought I could hear the sound still
    moving.
—Well, I have lied. Not so much lied as dreamed it.
I was three when he died. It was someone else—my sister—
went with him under the trees. But if it was her
memory then, it became mine so long since

I will owe nothing on it, having dreamed it from all
the nights I was growing, the wet-pants man of the family.
I have done nothing as perfect as I have dreamed him
from old-wives tales and the running of my blood.
God knows what queer long darks I had no eyes for

followed his stairwell weeks to his Sunday breezeways.
But I will swear the world is not well made that rips
such gardens from the week. Or I should have walked
a saint's way to the cross and nail by nail
hymned out my blood to glory, for one good reason.

Home Revisited: Midnight

I am the shadow in the shadow of the wicker.
The wicker is the shadow in the shadow of the vine.
I sat here when? Ago. Blinked in the flicker
Of a falling star. Said the moon: *Be mine.*
Said the star: *Will be.* And then, and now and then
The shadow in the shadow is the shadow of again.

And went away. Or came. What happened? O
It is June again and moony. *Song, song,*
So-ong, the crickets. And *blop, blop, b-lop*
The frogs. And *ago, ago, ago*
Says the rational man in the shadow. (This is his sop
To the passionate man in the song.) O do I belong
To that rational man? To that passionate singing man?
What body shall I wear to memory
When I arise from shadow?

Shall I cry Mother or write prose?
Turn Catholic or blow my nose?
If I rise and go inside
My dead setter will have died:
"Here, Tug. Here, Tug. Here on the lawn.
Here in the shadow." Tug is gone
To watch my shadow being born.

I was the center at the center of the shadow.
I am the shadow at the center of the thought.
The house behind me is a house I know,
At every sill and step the house forgot
All but *song, song, so-ong,* and *blop, blop, b-lop.*
That music is because it cannot stop.

37

For the center of the music is another music
And the center of the center is a stir.
And what is time that visited my father
With worms and roses and religious physic
And gave his house to me to sit and gather
Shadow at the center of the music of the stir?
And a rational man? And a passionate singing man?
And now,
        and then,
                a third, an invisible man
Singing and trusting and distrusting the song
At the center of the center where the shadows throng.

Something in the wild cherry—
the cat or another caution—
triggers the starlings and the tree
explodes. Who would have thought
so many pieces of life in one tree?
The air shakes with their whirligig.
The first have already lit across the field
before the last one's out.

They fling their bridge of lives
and of some sort of reason
across the field, a black
rainbow over my surprise.
What is it I prize in these commotions?
The burst of the live thing
takes me wholly to praise.
And if there are no gods

shaking the tree, as once
the father of man would have knelt
to omens, there is still
principle in his blood:
what goes is all going,
and all going graces
the true quick fact
a taken man is. I am

man again in their going.
Deep in the field of my coming
and of my father's coming

I stand taken
in this one rush
of lives upon us all.
What I had forgotten
was the suddenness of the real.

Now I remember
my mother wept for me
watching her man in this field
go slower and slower
while over him faster and faster
the wind shook out
the inexhaustible lives
that all life leaves.

The empty cherry quivers
in balance, spinning the light
inside itself. I had forgotten
how gradually the real is.
These two thoughts answer me:
between the exploded instant
and the long weather,
what walks the field is man.

Read down into the dead and close
tiers of the lying sand, soil, grass—
the root-sided, landsliding, unraisable
dawn and dark of the pit—
my stupid cousin, the missing
scholar of all, father of nothing, and boxer
who never won a fight,
lies dumb to the tears of women.

From the womb that stirred in dreams and soft
from dream dark coiled awake the son
of the man-touched, man-giving, and oh unholdable
sweet and milk of the flesh;
to dissolution and the swaying
censer like a pendulum under the timing sky;
the woman who was gifted
gives back her barren son.

He was the oaf of her litter, but not less
love's nor death's. Her better sons—
the un-needing, Sunday-visiting, check-writing
first felt of her blood—
stay her faint at the trembling sill;
but he was the last to need her and first
most gone from all morning
she held to her breasts' greatness.

While this one lived she had a child and was
mother to man. Childless, she sees him down
the flower-spilled, sand-back, and infolding ways

into the blood-black deep past
tears and time to the stone-stopped heart.
A pebble rattles there. The skirted priest
runs out of saints and ends. Her big sons turn her
back to the world where now she is their child.

i

After the living, the attic. Then the rain,
and children prowling indoors turned into the attic
to treasure-hunt the remains.

So Thursday when the wind turned.
Whistles blew: No school. No school.
Northeast from the Atlantic.

Rummage day under the eaves. The dressmaker's dummy
that was Aunt Clara welcomed us. The rain
scratched like a kitten. *Let's play store.*

Not much imagination but let them be.
Sea-blown kittens over aunty's ghost
change no habits. They *like* to play store.

Then Jenny brings me the album she bought for two papers.
"Look! Look at the man in the funny hat!"
—Hello, Father.

Is heaven the cave above us, under the rafters
aged the color of leather? The dead are dusty
everywhere we touch them. Jenny brings me

Paul at three in his grandmother's lap:
the gray-leather smile at the suede child I think
means nothing. Age is no skill but a nuisance.

43

Store it away.
The rain is its own arrival. It needs nothing.
If accident follow the act, is that an action?

Yes, Jenny, it must go back.
The faces need their time, as time needs faces.
Someday even Jenny will need to be sad

as great grandmother's talons on the child,
as Aunt Clara's dummy, as father's easy thirties
in a funny hat.

But oh, Mother, what eyes my father had!

ii

Order? The son of the man beside his children
has no other. Why should I teach them the rain
who know already they can play in it?
Now they are dressing the dummy in old curtains.
Well, what if Aunt Clara's heaped in one more dust rag?
father's a laugh in a derby?—let them be:

time's for a time. I'm here to beg not preach.

iii

Fingers drum on the roof. *Ratapan, ratapan, ratapan.*
Snakes writhe on the sea.
                              And the big wind.
Ratapan. For the dilatory man.
For the literary, tutelary

capillary man.

I know no artery to the dead nor vein dark
as the Cretan's river:
                          a smallest mesh
webs Uncle Cesar to his handlebars
(very gay nineties)
                          and the great stance
seeming to say: "Throw me a live bull; I'm hungry."
No more. It's after dinner.
                          And Father again,
with Mother a beauty beside him; this man's woman
in the flower time of starting:
                          veils, smiles,
initiation rituals—the solid seeming
places of the tribe.
                          And Father's father,
photographer- and Sunday-scrubbed and scarved,
Sorrento painted behind him
                          Con affetto
al mio figlio lontano. And over his ear
a rip in the photographer's Sorrento.
                          Canvas too
turns to a leathery dust. A dusty sea
sneezes in the wind.
                          Clara, Cesar, Lorenzo.
Licked by the flaming children. Felice, Cristina.
Ratapan, ratapan, ratapan,
                          for the fritillary man.

        iv
And the Sunday paper. Last Sunday's.

Already an archive under the pitched roof.
THE ROYAL LIFE ON THE PORTUGUESE RIVIERA.
FOG ENDANGERS JERSEY TURNPIKE.
DIOCLETIAN PONDERS DIVIDED EMPIRE.
P. VERGILIUS MARO PREDICTS CHRIST.
DANGER OF GLACIER SEEN AVERTED.

Tom Ferril. That's his trick for a World Edition
of a One Star Final.
He wants to publish a paper for Mount Massive.
Well, haven't I stolen more than that. Or begged it?—
Have an emotion for me: let me live:
shall I need less than a child the child's perfection
at rummage under the rafters? Let any man store me.

—And so the temptation to prayer. The exultant refusal
to let the dead go dusty under the rain.
Men have missed death but worms have eaten them
in love with life.—And there's another steal.
As the children must be stolen
out of my father's archives. Traveler's gear
forgotten in the dust of a lighted fog.

V

And what road?
"The Turnpike's record to date stands
at 5.8 fatalities per
100,000,000 vehicle miles,
As compared to a national average
of 7.6." As compared—
to what?

At an average rate
of 11 miles per hour the Tiber flows
96,426,000 miles per millennium,
with a record to date of
one civilization.
           Over the Tiber,
looking down from the Ponte del Risorgimento,
I saw a hawk float by.
Not a reflection in the sky.
The bird itself in its own death,
wings outspread on the water,
clouded by flies in its going,
a nebula.
           The stars are no further
over Sioux Falls than over the Colliseum.
In Jersey City
I saw the day-moon over the wood
of the video aerials. When I entered the Turnpike
the fog came. By Entrance Eleven
the wreck waited. The corpse grinned out of metal.

    vi

And the rain. The rain.
Pattering the car top.
Coming too fast for the wiper.
My daughter slept at my back
in a portable bed.
The ambulance came
for tidiness only.
There was nothing left to save.

The dead man lay
openly in the rain.
Morbid, I waited,
pleased by my own revulsion.
The man is dead
when the rain falls openly.
There are roofs on the living.
His rain is another sound.

For him the box is ripped.
The kittens have scratched it.
The flies await their constellations vainly.
The river is stone to the crematorium;
the embalmed vein, a solid.
There is nothing the stars
may gnaw in their swarms
but dark.

vii

Muddle, muddle, muddle, says the rain
on the roof. The sea's hissing.
The fog's stuck to the world.
Somewhere a bank gulps gone.

So Thursday among the children who do not see
days but games, places but games.
A singleness of the blood at its round flowing.
Why play at less than life?

Muddle, muddle, muddle, says the rain.
Roundness is all. The round game like a music:

the first sound calling the second into being.
Lightly, lightly, *graziosamente*. Follow the music

into itself. A road like any other.
Past children in the rain, past the stone news,
beyond the rip in the old man's Sorrento.
Ratapan. For the cinerary man.

But oh, children, what eyes our father had!

A Variation on Some Lines

Muddle, muddle, muddle, says the rain.
I hear the river hissing.
The fog's stuck to the window.
Somewhere a bank gulps gone.

A time of no shape. I feel the mountains
hurry. Trees go loose in the air.
The sound of the clock comes out of the hallway
and holds: *bat, bat, bat, bat.*

I meant a praise. A form. In a calm unease
I dread for all things made.
Muddle, muddle, muddle, says the rain.
The fog's stuck to the world.

And a rain stain on the ceiling blooms
two perfect suggestions: rose and fish.
What's art when wet plaster's
subtler than Yves Tanguy?

I'll make a praise:
is chance or the eye the shape?
do the bones of the carp know
how prayerfully China has drawn them?

What's seen is saved.
What's heard is answered.
Beat, beat, beat, says the blood.
Light, says the eye, *Pray me.*

When Willie Crosby died I thought too much:
Sister and Mother and Uncle and Father O'Brien
All talked about me and how
It was all very touching: *Such sorrow.*
He really lived in that boy.
Here now, you gowonoff to the movies.
Give your grief to God.

But here I am in Missouri twenty years later
Watching the rain come down
That no one prayed for: a drowned crop
And the Mississippi rising
On a wet world still washing away the kid
Who thought too much about Willie Crosby
But went to the movies all the same.
It was a lovely wake and everyone admired me.

At night the Salt Hills go blue perfectly.
Having survived a theology and a war,
I am beginning to understand
The rain.

To My Father

Watching the gulls precisely as you too
Have watched them salt the distance of the wind
Through a mare's tail sky over granite and granite water,

I could toss any pebble from this cliff
or pop it into my mouth like Demosthenes
to practice whatever is practiced by serious persuaders.

But how, having tasted stone, does any man
return from it? I have tasted the earth of that pebble.
I cannot believe very much in sincerity.

I could preach to the wallowing wind: I had a Father:
Where is he now? A big Italian man
loaded me on this shore and left me laughing

with the taste of his stone in my mouth. I praise these gulls
with the blood of every rape that stored my fathers:
Greek, Turk, Moor, Hun, Goth, Visigoth—what else?—

up from Salerno the riding Englishman
with money for a villa, shaking the air
when the girl was gone with morning and his money.

When her child was born she bought him seven goats
from the pouch in her breasts and the bastard walked them
    laughing
under the gulls and over his fatherless hills

singing the song of the two sons he was,
of the robber and the robbed, but knowing only
the one tongue of his cheeses and his milk.

Here I sit, all proper, right-handed and legal,
but as much my father's stranger as ever he was.
—They told me I look like you. But for what reason?

Perhaps, I think, to sit here over the water
remembering what we were before we changed.
Or to account, perhaps, for what laughter the light is

over the fins of the fish and the shins of the drowned
and the waters under Genesis spreading away
from the coal-black edge of winter in the rock,

here at the shore of this steepled and proper New England
whose history is also finished, leaving no Rome
to stand from the hills, but only the Irishman's Boston,

and a legend of virtue that took the boat for Paris;
through the Louvre with a guidebook, through the Quai with
   a checkbook
to ginger the walls and mantels of Beacon Hill.

Here on my fatherless hills as the bastard sat
easy on his, watching his seven goats cropping,
I think we have been had in all good humor

you and I, hearing the laughter come bubbling
out of the earth like springs and its waters flowing
sweet as flutes over the easy-going

dip of the poppies' noon by a stone ruin.
What are you doing there sulking under the breakjaw
and final stone wedged in the orator's mouth?

—Let laughter damn me easy. My father's skinny,
but the goats have tended the bastard and multiplied
milk into cheeses and the cheese to song

he spilled to the lifted gulls, as once they spilled
high from the wind on a sea-berating Greek,
Old Logos with a bird turd on his bald spot.

Three Views of a Mother

i

Good soul, my mother holds my daughter,
the onion-skin bleached hand under the peach-head.
Ti-ti, she says from the vegetable world, *la-la*.
A language of roots from a forgotten garden.

She forms like a cresting wave over the child;
it is impossible not to see her break
and bury and the child swim up a girl
and the girl reach shore a woman on my last beach.

Ti-ti, la-la. I will not fight our drowning,
nor the fall of gardens. I am curious, however,
to know what world this is. The honey-dew head
of the child, the cauliflower head of the grandmother

bob in the sea under the garden. *Ti-ti, la-la*.
The grandmother rustles her hands like two dry leaves
and the child writhes round as a slug for pleasure,
leaving the trail of its going wet on the world.

ii

I see her in the garden, loam-knuckled in Spring,
urging the onions and roses up. Her hands
talk to the shoots in whispers, or in anger
they rip a weed away between thumb and fist.

When the jonquils open she makes a life of them.
Before the radishes come she is off to the fields,

scarved and bent like a gleaner, for dandelions.
When the beans are ready she heaps them in a bowl.

The Fall is lit by peaches. As if they were bubbles
she balances them from the branch and holds them out
one by one in her palm. Her eyes believe
the world self-evident in its creation.

Last of all the chrysanthemums take tongue
from the spikes of November. She lingers by glass boxes
coaxing the thickened earth a little longer
to hoard the sun for sprigs of mint and parsley.

But Winter comes and she is out of employment
and patience. She is not easy to be with
here by the buried garden. Winter mornings
she wakes like shrouded wax, already weary

of the iron day. *Ti-ti*, she says to the child,
la-la. A piece of her life. But her mind divides:
she knows there is seed enough for every forest,
but can she be sure there is time for one more garden?

iii

Three rainy days and the fourth one sunny:
she was gone before breakfast. At three she hobbles back
under a flour sack bulging full of mushrooms.
Well, scolding will do no good. I see her eyes
hunting for praise as she fishes up a handful
and holds them to the light, then rips one open
for me to smell the earth in the white stem.

I think perhaps this woman is my child.
But right now what do we do with thirty pounds
of uncleaned mushrooms? If I let her be
she'll stay up cleaning them till one o'clock
and be all aches tomorrow. I get a knife;
and here we sit with the kitchen table between us,
one pile for root ends, one for the cleaned sprouts.

Her hands go back with her. I see her mind
open through fields from the earth of her stained fingers.
"Once when I was a girl I found a fungus
that weighed twenty-eight kilos. It was delicious.
I was going to Benevento for the fair.
I cut across the mountain to save time,
and there it was—like an angel in a tree.

"You don't see things like that. Not over here.
My father ran from the barn when I came home.
'Didn't you go to fair?' he said. But I laughed:
'I brought it home with me.' He wouldn't believe
I'd carried it all the way across the mountain,
and the path so steep. I made a sack of my skirt.
He thought some fellow—I don't know what he thought!"

Ti-ti. La-la. The memory works her fingers.
"Oh, we were happy then. You could go in the winter
and dig the roses and cabbages from the snow.
The land had a blessing. In the fall in the vineyards
we sang from dawn to sunset, and at night
we washed our feet and danced like goats in the grape vats.
The wine came up like blood between our toes."

57

We finish at last, the squid-gray fruit before us.
"Leave the root clippings," she says. "They're for the garden.
See how black the dirt is. Black's for growing."
She sets her hoard to soak. "I'm tired now.
Sometimes I talk too much. That's happiness.
Well, so we'll eat again before we die.
But oh, if you could have seen it in that tree!"

Poem for My Thirty-Ninth Birthday

Itchy with time in the dogday summer stew,
    flesh melting at its creases and salted raw,
I drove the day for breezes. The children blew
    kisses to traffic. In the stubbly jaw
of the bay my wife went wading. In the wood
    a mouse lay torn on stone beside a pool,
an anthill raging in him like a mood
    of the dogday, a weather of the soul.

Waiting by pools for the fish that spins all water
    and the mouse that will come. Steaming on lawns
in a tinkle of gin. Spraying my birdy daughter,
    my guppy-bubbling son, and nodding like bones
on the leash of love, I heard the wind go over
    like jet-scream, the fact gone before the sound
ripped at the world. And naked as a lover
    I watched a pointed moon sprout from the ground.

It was too thin to die to. Fat as meat,
    I stood alive into my thirty-ninth year
from the deaddog day of summer, the shag heat
    still matted like wet wool on the midnight air,
and took my death for reason. Here it was
    the red worm pushed a nerve-end onto rock.
The world began with women in the house,
    and men with wine jugs waiting on the walk.

Over and through the reefs the thin moon skids,
    the great squid of the storm squirts down the air.

A clam of light glints out of swollen lids.
        Flying fish leap at the barrier.
There goes the moon, shipwrecked on churning stone.
        What holds the weather up? A raging Morse
flickers along the reef. Let down! Let down!
        But the moon rides up and holds, dead to its course.

A specimen ego pokes into the hour—
        news from the sea my mother's screaming broke.
I ate her in her pain. Manchild and sour
        from the sea's gland, I sweetened as I woke
out of her milk. But if the land was love,
        it was half-terror and too big to dare.
In a great plain, the ticking grass above
        my head and reach, I waited with my ear

to the thudding ground. What passed me out of sight?
        My father was one. When I had died enough
I made a perfect pink boy of my fright
        and used him to forgive time and myself.
Thirty-nine dying birthday years behind,
        he listens at the children's sleep and goes
sighing with love and pity to the blind
        and breathing love's-bed at the long thought's close.

Here in the thought, outside my house in time,
        the year comes where it is. I watch it down
under a moon rubbed like a garlic spline
        to a last skin. The river, thick as stone

sweats beads out of the air. A waiting man,
    itchy with time and damp as I was born,
I count my birthdays grave by grave, and stand
    watching the weather tremble to the storm

that cooked all day while I strolled death by death
    by pools, by lawns, by sea, and all my loves.
Time as it is. A laboring to breath
    in the clogged air. A nudging at what shoves.
A tapping at what blows. A waiting still
    at the sweet fear and bittering appetite.
A ghost that will not and a ghost that will
    burn faster as it burns out of the night

where all men are their fathers and their sons
    in a haunted house of mirrors to the end.
I have walked my deaths out of a day of bones
    and put my loves to bed, and free, and found
in the laboring summer flesh of man, I wait
    easy enough for the lit nerve and hover
of thunderheads to bolt the moon and break
    the stuck air open, like a death blown over.

POEMS LOOKING OUT

Gnostic Faustus, Sapphic, sophic,
the face set firm but the eyes Orphic,
dream-dead eyes, eyes brought blind
from a world too-many, eyes of the mind
of Faustus, all that crazy imagination
of fruit out of season, and of course a Mädchen,
and of course the devil behind a column,
very basso, very solemn . . .

Who knows Faustus? Houris? Horrors?
What's that scratching? Fates? Furies?
Who's that coming through the floor?—
the Queen of Maggots or the Girl Next Door?
Who's in the mind of Faustus? the big, overacted,
nightmare-lashing, perpetually erect, tom-tom impacted
mind of Faustus? Is Faustus true?
Is he in me? Is he in you?

Dapper Faustus, deft, demonic,
manic, monocle-Germanic.
What's in the mind of Faustus? the cracked,
hand-rubbing, cackle-ridden, thunder-backed,
blown mind of Faustus way up there
at the top of his tower, at the top of the air?
And all that world spread at his feet
does he need it all? Is Need his fate?

Leach Faustus, learned lecher,
Don of Puberty, devil-fetcher;
Faustus ranting in a dim green light;

a mind like New Haven on a Saturday night,
or Poe in the suburbs, or Marlowe's Jew,
rakehell, rankle, or bad homebrew.
Whiffenpoof Faustus or Manfred or maddened,
but singing damnation till he wished he hadn't.

Then ptotic Faustus, caustic, clastic,
phthisic, acrotic, kataplastic;
grimoire, grimalkin, and an amber skull
grouped on his desk, the pentacle
limed on his floor, and death outside,
death afire like a panther's hide,
heaving and straining but held by the spell.
Till one line breaks. Then home to hell . . .

"He over-reached," the whisper slips
from wizard to witch, the flaking lips
of demons smirk, the saved and bleached
cluck in the rafters. "He over-reached."
So Faustus turns the page and falls
out of the tower, a million bells
shiver as one to watch him go.
Even Faustus knows Faustus now.

Then up the music and down the curtain:
"Misbehave and you're damned for certain."
"If you haven't got Luther you'd better get Peter,
or somebody else gets Margherita."
"Watch out for salesmen with black goatees:
one of them's Mephistopheles."

"And stay away from the cellar door
or you'll end up like the Herr Doktor."

But what of Faustus? Poor sick Faustus. Faustus going
down for a moral. Everyone knowing
all about Faustus, taught about Faustus, mad, bad, sin-
ful, witchbrewed, uncontainable, all-dissolving, skin-
and-bones Faustus, who could have lived fat
and been a judge and a Geheimrat.
But couldn't find anyone whose conversation
was less damnation than Damnation.

Childe Horvald to the Dark Tower Came

Well, they loaded him with armor and left him
All night by the altar rail, and he was young,
And darks have voices when you pray to hear them,
And in the morning his lord unbuckled
And blessed his shoulder, and most were drunk yet
From the night wassail, and all the girls. . . .

At, say, sixteen can you doubt the dark and the girls?
The grail, they told him, *the grail.* And he: *I swear it.*

And so the tower rose beyond his dead horse
In the valley of drifted bones. He blew his horn then
(Noise of the true man), and unbuckled, and came twirling
The folderol sword hilted with girls' garlands
And of course *Blut und Ehre* sloganed on it,
And worse nonsense brave in his head.

                        And what would you
Do if you were the magician hearing
His boy-murderous blast shaking your phials and silences,
Watching him come shouting *St. Poobah and the dragon!*
Into your library and uncertainty?

                       It takes
More than civility to civilize
The very young. I say send out a peri
If you've her address or her incantation,
Or drug him if you can, or conjure him on
To the bog of his own idiocy. But for Godsake

Don't let him into the house with his nice profile

All tensed for swordplay and lifting of heads
At arm's length over the fallen books.

Or if you've real
Magic, change him! change him!

A Box Comes Home

I remember the United States of America
As a flag-draped box with Arthur in it
And six marines to bear it on their shoulders.

I wonder how someone once came to remember
The Empire of the East and the Empire of the West.
As an urn maybe delivered by chariot.

You could bring Germany back on a shield once
And France in a plume. England, I suppose,
Kept coming back a long time as a letter.

Once I saw Arthur dressed as the United States
Of America. Now I see the United States
Of America as Arthur in a flag-sealed domino.

And I would pray more good of Arthur
Than I can wholly believe. I would pray
An agreement with the United States of America

To equal Arthur's living as it equals his dying
At the red-taped grave in Woodmere
By the rain and oakleaves on the domino.

The stone wheel running in the weeds
Crushes the quail's egg with a sound of time.
I see the phosphorescent teeth of the dead
In a new Asia. Ivy and barbed wire climb
Rotundas of a skull. The surf throws up
A shale of eyes. And fingers walk alone
      Out of the sand.

A gull at the bombed bomb-dump blows
Into a cloud and falls as rain. It rains
Into the sea and grasses and down through stone
The rain goes dark to dirty wells and dark
To the seepage of the hills. You think perhaps
Death's in the crust: death's in the core of stone,
      Part of a tension

And adjustment of depths: there were
Too many fingers and we snapped them, too many
Eggs, eyes and we squashed them, too
Many gulls and we blew them to rain for
There is too much waiting to change
In a man's life. So we changed that. We changed
      All our waiting,

And will not wait again for green
Or grace or grief. For the dead take too long
To bury: there are too many waiting: we must learn
How to take gulls apart so thoroughly
There's only rain left, how to make eyes fingers mouths
Of the invisible event a man is
      Behind his distance.

At a Concert of Music,
REMEMBERING THE DEAD IN KOREA

Consider says the music how man is an age
Waiting to be discovered. This is a question
But its answer is a delay, the delay is
The answer. Consider says the trembling of the sound
What echoes are in a man. His lives spend
His lives like music; all unknown till heard
Yet everywhere expected, known in the hearing
And in the hearing recognized as precisely
What he had waited to hear. Until at last,
What have the dead become in their surprises?

The postures of the dead, the trembling sings,
Are all familiar. None remain to discover
But only to occur, sighs the organ.
In the documentary ditch by the newsreel road
The cramped, the outflung, the piled over and under
Melt together like sound, whispers the cello.
Parts of a world contrived beyond surprises,
The oboe, the failing bassoon, the mottled flute.
Nothing follows but the music the music:
Do you really imagine you can hear a silence?

When the trumpets invaded Russia the drums struck,
The fifes screeched on the ice, the cymbals broke
From snow steppe and pine cover. Then like a bass
The ice rocked and the fiddles drowned in the rivers.
The bows washed to Latvia and the bridges
To Estonia. The heart-shaped bodies warped
Open in Polish weeds. Then Spring was all harps

In the wind over the brassland where the movement
Fought and died, fought and died and was never
Ended, cannot end.

                    For how shall the dead
Exist who are a silence behind the sound
Whereby silence is an impossibility?
There is dying again in the ditches, says the music,
But I have heard myself in my beginning:
How shall I be surprised who have no surprises?
Consider says the music how man must be
His own delay and answer. His own secretion
Like music of his lives about his lives,
Says the fall and the fading, says the echo between
The hearts of the fiddles invisibly trembling together.

A Thought About Shiek Bedreddin

I read in a tattered book about Shiek Bedreddin
who on his best day sank ten thousand axes
into the Royal Heir's ranks, and broke eight thousand.
Men, that is. Snapped brittle at the handle
for what's crazy in everyone. Called a glory.
With, of course, a gallows. Some want *that* badly
to be taken in righteousness. Of Shiek Bedreddin,
it is written he was hanged between two rivers
preaching firm faith to his two thousand "survivors,"
their heads under their arms in strict attention.

Now there's a day's work: ten thousand wraith
decisions sopped up into history
like garlic gravy, leaving a bad breath
somewhere among the back smells of Turkey,
and everywhere. The slops did very well
the day Bedreddin preached the way to hell
to his last two thousand rags of crazy cloth.
I almost wish I knew what they thought they were doing
aside from that day's immediate hacking and hewing.
There must be something to say of that much death.

Ship's bells of faith at altar ports
Ring for the voyager. One candle power
Lighthouses warn him from the rock and wreck,
The seas divide on a star's altitude,
And every port is known. He ships his gear
Of beads and bones, climbs gangways made of light.

Now see the mast ringed with St. Elmo's fire,
Aurora of the four-dimensioned soul.
God has the sailing list, the wireless code,
The state department cipher, the mine-field chart.
His semaphore has quarantined the damned.
His turbines throb the decks of secret speed runs.

Buoys to windward toll the world's last look:
A neon shore line, a blast furnace glare
Not Hell nor Pittsburgh, but the political damned
Shriek from the docks, guilty of all their sins,
Of birth and wish. The voyager stands firm:
"In His will is our freedom. Forgive my vote."

Now past the legal limit on high seas
Bound only by a round infinity
The biscuit and the cup are passed about,
The watch is set, the helmsman picks a star,
And some rip down the wireless from the world
On secret orders from the speaking tube.

On these proverbial seas where no land bird
Or shore-green wreckage drifts, his journal reads

A voyage to himself: "My doubts are gone.
The ocean is my peace. Today I threw
My shore clothes overboard. The captain smiled.
I shudder at my memories and feel free."

In the Witch-Hunting Season

I tell you, don't trust the living. Their eyes
go mad for practice. They're possessed, possessing.
Give them one good Friday and they're up and ready

with nails and religions. Hysteria's their mother.
There's a scratch in them that won't heal.
They have twelve fingers sticky with bleeding.

Get thin. Put by some dying before you're owned
hock shank and marrow, and out nailing Jews
for fat reasons. Get a grave behind you.

What else made the Sahara a saints' suburb
and singed the mob at the city gates when the bones
strolled back as easy as gypsies, all their own?

Ask Ezra at St. Elizabeth's mismanaging
a dozen languages in a rage of tricks
to pile all Hells into one dictionary.

Ask Blake head first in the tiger's mouth. Ask Donne
being bad for God. Ask Byron being bad.
Ask Dr. Johnson what he's doing dead

when grammar's cracking wider every day—
paid-in-full Lazarus, the one safe
man in all dangerous Judea, is my saint.

Kristófer Second

for Fletcher Pratt

Kristófer the Second, by Grace of God
King of the Danes, crowned on the hill
By Denmark's law, died in a ditch
Grated by Germans. Sing we his saga:

Loud from Lohede echoed the clanging
Of blades and ambitions: the clatter of kings
Hacking through mist, their vision of standing
Erect above time, a rock in water.

Then reeling in rout, hurry of horses,
Wheels on the nights ways, shivered ambition.
Alone in his lodge and sullen with sleep
He dreamed of the devil, Graf Johann the Mild:

Woke all a-startle, smoke for his sidewalls,
Flames for his hangings. Under the window
Two knights with a net hauled him like herring,
Loaded him laughing, Graf Johann's catch,

Brought to his breakfast. "How shall we serve him?"
Graf Johann sat grinning: "Too thin a sprat:
Strip him and whip him out of the gate
And bring me a fish with flesh to its bones."

Loud was the laughter of knouts through the air,
The dancing of horses dragging his dust.
At the fork of the road they cut his cord:
A garrison's joke grew stale in the ditch.

The boy-king of nettles died weeping for water;
His blood lay about him too dirty to drink.
From Sylt to Skaane, from Loeso to Lübeck
There was none found to bury a king.

And down from the turrets of Skanderborg
The ravens rode to their black Thing
Wide on the weeds to pick and pick.
May God forgive all politic.

Elegy for G. B. Shaw

"If I survive this, I shall be immortal."

Administrators of minutes into hours,
Hours into ash, and ash to its own wedding
At the edge of fire and air—here's time at last
To make an ash of Shaw, who in his time
Survived his times, retired, and for a hobby
Bred fire to fire as one breeds guinea pigs.

In time, one can imagine, schoolchildren
Will confuse him as a contemporary of Socrates.
For a time, the fact is, he confused us:
We half believed he really had lived forever.
Sometimes, perhaps, a man can. That is to say,
Civilization is one man at a time,

And that forever, and he was that man.
For this we will not forgive him. Neither
The ape in me nor the ape in you, tenants
Of the flag-flying tree and drinkers of blood in season.
We meant to resemble the agonies of statues:
He left us only a treadmill in a cage.

Consider his crimes: He would not commit our diet.
He opened our tombs. He sold his medals for cash.
His laughter blew out our anthems. He wiped his nose
On the flags we die for—a crazy Irishman
Who looked like a goat and would not be serious.
But when we are finished, he will be our times.

And all times will be nothing in his eye.
All marshals, kings, and presidents we obey.

His presence in men's minds is contempt of court,
Of congress, and of flags. So must we pray
That he be born again, anarch and rare,
The race we are not in the race we are.

The Invasion of Sleep Walkers

(What I shall say to my Father)

They were weeding out the dead at the funeral home
to reduce the overstock. Rack after rack
the wire-hung bones chattered their loneliness
and even the drunkenest angel wept and sang.
But the coroner's men were stuffed too full for hearing,
the trucks were backed to the wind, and the sleep walkers
already were pacing the streets, their eyes like spit,
their arms out stiff before them, their knees unbending,
their heels hitting too hard. They had no faces,
or, more exactly, they had the look of faces
that could not happen or that had not happened —
once on Fifth Avenue I watched five miles
of faceless cops march on St. Patrick's day
and learned that face forever —
                                There's not much more:
when the dead had been thinned out they put that face
over the skulls and gave them back to us.
We marched all day and night with flags and torches
to celebrate our thanks. The Great Good Face
stared down from photographs ten stories high.
It had no eyes but it saw my guilt at once
among a million marchers. I never learned
what signal passed between it and the Law,
but something certainly — and here I am.

Can Hell be taken more seriously than the world?

I Thanked the Lunatic for a Particular View

Happy with recognition, I saw the voltage
of the madman's hair erect and his eyes
like two burned fuses. In his mislaid rage
the world lay scalped at the poles and skies
the color of eggplant spilled out stars like seed
where they lay split by his nagging. I agreed
there was no more tragedy, only that drift of news
over the planets striped like croquet balls.
And pleased indeed, I thought how like a shoe
with broken tongue and laces, his brown jowls
worked the world away in the flip-flopping
void and abyss through which the stars were dropping.

Lines for Woodlawn

Good men have wandered into death mistaken:
captains have missed a curve and kings a hint,
skippers have watched all night and raised no beacon,
skiers have drifted off the edge like lint.

At Woodlawn's Gates of Heaven scream the jays
in the soapstone shade of spruce, a butterfly
burns on a bud, a chipmunk pops and goes
from sods where good men shed. And who am I

to keep the books of heaven to a prayer
or write the ticket to their bins of bones?
Good men lie damned where good men lay before:
when Heaven needs clerks it has this field of stones.

PRAYERS

Temptation

Volgiti indietro, e tien lo viso chiuso:
chè, se il Gorgon si mostra, e tu il vedessi,
nulla sarebba del tornar mai suso.

St. Anthony, my father's holy man,
was tempted by a worm-shop, spills of guts,
soft coupling toads, blind fish, and seeing maggots.
The whores the devil sent leaked through their skin.

Now who would leave off heaven for such stuff?
What in the devil was the devil thinking
to try to turn a man with such a stinking
parcel of shoddy? Or were times so tough

he hadn't one small kingdom, or at least
one final Lilith to give sin some standing
a man could sell his soul for without branding
himself a damn fool before man and beast?

The devil's a better fisherman than angels
or he'd have starved long since. When slobs die poor
on rotten kingdoms and a nagging whore
still in her heat when every other chills,

the devil keeps that last bait for the ardent:
my father bit bare iron to go damned:
I see the leakage past the door he slammed:
I think the devil almost hooked his saint.

Flowering Quince

This devils me: uneasy ease at my window
  discussing the day with quince, flowers of the quince
  almost upon me in tree time, in slow
  dazzles of budding and bending asprawl since
    Spring began my consideration again

of the angels of the blind eye. *This must mean*
  the angels sing from the many-folded falls
  of the open light, from the twist and gnarl and sheen
  of the airy works of the tree, from the writhen scrawls
    and mobile arms of its tilt and balancing.

But at once the wind shakes free a fall of light
  from undiminished light, the light-machine
  sends and goes in an ample-handed sleight.
  This devils me: can worlds be made to mean
    whatever they are about when they shape a tree?

can the angel-blinded eye be made to enter
  a presence without intent whose devils sprawl
  calmer than angels in the windborne center
  of the quince-bursting Spring? is quince a moral?
    The form of a tree is a function of the air

and its only possibility, say the devils.
  But the eye sees by religions and recollections.
  What shall the green bough care for rites and revels
  or the angel imagination whose paeons
    moralize the strictness of God's chains

in a world that cannot worship but only answer
one urgency with another? Spring
is no more intricately bloomed than cancer,
nor than the dreams of angels which they fling
age after age at the invincible world.

Sunday Morning

I light a cigarette, my dead mouth steaming
    with vapors of its own. One jellied eye
    splits out of sleep, and blood comes up from dreaming
    in poisoned wells, while the bell-driven sky
    scuds to St. Joseph's just across the river
    calling the Sunday Irish, hands together,
    to walk the incensed aisle of the Forgiver
    under His eye, His steeple, and His ringing weather.

A sip of coffee muddies on my tongue
    and metal citrus savors how it is
    to taste the melting wafer there among
    the arches of the God. If I were his
    would I wake sweeter? Suddenly there leaps,
    like a dancer bursting naked from her cloak,
    a swell of sun, and on the cloud that sleeps
    up from the ashtray rears Our Lady of Lit Smoke.

Saints have seen less and gone with it to grace.
    For such a light Nazarius lost his head
    to the prefect Anolinus. It was Ambrose
    who found the grave. As de Voragine said:
    "From it there came a perfume wondrous sweet."
    Those old ones had an easy way with graves.
    I wallow in the grave of my own meat,
    watching the light exult, golden as all their *Ave*'s.

Ah well, I think, I shall not want at last
    for the comic operas of the saint. I read
    how Brixius charged with fornication passed

two miracles to prove him pure indeed.
Yet was he driven by an angry mob
for having called St. Martin an old fool.
So are all driven, but will the holy squab
testify for all before the Sunday School?

. . . A music for the images of Sunday
under the ray that does if any will
to be Godmother to the light. I play
these rummages toward grace under the spill
of overflowing Heaven. The fat man's prayer
is an easy going random: I will raise
what images arrive across this air
until the sour of time be sweetened into praise.

The warrior image: Nelson in Sicily
drummed up a war to please the Hamilton whore,
and when he captured old Prince Carracioli
hanged him from a yardarm just offshore
then dropped him over. The next day at tea,
the cabin windows open and the old bag
passing the rum, the corpse broke from the sea
and stared out of blind eyes at the hero and his hag.

(I wonder if those blood-tubs ever banged
for better stuff. Sometimes I think I mean
it's better to be Carracioli hanged
than Nelson diddled. And wasn't Josephine
another whore?—There's Empire from both ends!—
I hear my teeth grind in the toast I chew

and ponder through what fogs the squab descends
there where the Irish eat their Christ and hate the Jew.

A moral for the images of Sunday:
    I think the world is less than its own light
    aureoled on the smoke that sleeps away
    from a fat man's cigarette and morning rite.
    What have they ever won but marzipan
    from Mother Mush or from the sticky lips
    of such a tub as Hamilton, who man
    the artilleries of God aboard his battering ships?)

The rhetorical image: Voltaire at sixty-one
    wrote out a quarrel with the Lisbon earthquake
    in the name of human dignity. Half a town
    fell into its dark before it came awake,
    because a mountain shrugged. And one old comic
    (the victim of too much philosophy?)
    dipped his pen in blood for a polemic,
    declaiming for the mind against sheer casualty.

The silly image: Perillus, a smith of Athens,
    delivered to Phalaris of Sicily
    a brazen bull so tuned by cunning engines
    that when a man was toasted in its belly
    his dying screams were changed into a Moo.
    The king smiled and the smith was first to sing.
    Later Phalaris fell and then he too
    warmed into song to please the humors of a king.

Mother Illusion, Mary of Lit Time,
   how sweetly gone they flicker and have done!
   Dante brought the Universe to rhyme
   in such a light. I sort out one by one
   these pebbles from a beach of space and pray
   from finite stuff some infinite gentleness
   to offer the soft air and the bright Sunday
   that joys the heavy man at play with his distress.

Ghost of All Shining, Vowel of Light
   which rings my bones, gross in their morning-stale,
   I dream the swollen doe gone mad with fright
   when the hounds bell for her fawn. I dream the whale
   anguished with milky love on the grating shoal,
   the dove at the cat-shorn nest, the bitch in snow
   by the dead man. My Lady Aureole
   who are the gentlest man becomes, his good of sorrow—

these beasts are breathed out of my nearest wish.
   For joy of them, bright mother, I pray let down
   your shining on bird, beast, and fish
   till all things live, and all things lack conviction
   of all but light. A fat man breathes this prayer
   in sight of skinny death who teaches all
   the joy man breathes from the blood burning air,
   and that man stands most tall measured against his tall.

Measurements

I've zeroed an altimeter on the floor
then raised it to a table and read *three feet*.
Nothing but music knows what air is
more precisely than this. I read on its face
Sensitive Altimeter and believe it.

Once on a clear day over Arkansas
I watched the ridges on the radar screen,
then looked down from the blister and hung like prayer:
the instrument was perfect: ridge by ridge
the electric land was true as the land it took from.

These, I am persuaded, are instances
round as the eye to see with,
perfections of one place in the visited world
and omens to the godly
teaching an increase of possibility.

I believe that when a civilization
equal to its instruments is born
we may prepare to build such cities as music
arrives to on the air, lands where we are
the instruments of April in the seed.

i

Tricodon of Bruges, a Flemish
Poet of no reputation and
Of no talent but tears,
Wept into his inkwell
All one night, then hanged himself—
His only gift to the dawn.

ii

Aldo, the tragedian of Padua,
Was another weeper. Passion in him
Invited all accident. Sandbags
Rained on his love scenes, flies
Wavered on his battles, the doors of his castles
Fell on him when he bolted them.

iii

Malorca of Galicia was another.
A defender. Shot at his wife's lover
And killed the General's palomino.
He left his tears on a wall in Estremadura:
God grant me sustenance within myself
To bear the dirty chuckle of the wind.

iv

Sophia of Montenegro died naked in a pie
On her way to the Duke's table. Her own
Golden surprise for him. But he
Was dining in his chambers with La Guernerra
When his firebird sank through its gilding
Under the lorgnette of the Countess Merla.

95

V

To remember what has never been is not
To lie but to read the future:
A place in nature where Pollonius the pincushion
Stitched into a tapestry of Clichy
Speaks into Van Gogh's ear, and all perceive
The action of incorrigible farce.

Fragment of a Bas Relief

The knife, the priest, the heifer
Wander stonily into shadows of erosion,
Profiles of gem-eyed Egypt.

How shall I ever believe the world is real?

Carlo Crivelli Muses Before a Madonna

ΦBK Poem   Harvard   1952

i

"Impiety!" they scream. Impiety!
Because I sent a fly to shine beside her!
Was it not God who made the fly a jewel?

What would they have me paint to honor her? —
the great laps of their mothers? I pray delight.
I pray the adorations I have learned

setting before her a sufficient place
between the world and what we love—not objects
but the presence of the object in her look.

ii

I dream the Idea of the Lady—a separation
of all she is from all that nature is.
Nature can only visit her attention

asking for its perfection in her look,
praying to be completed to itself
in the arrest and random of her eye:

to the peach its swollen light, to the fly its jewel,
to her distracted hands the wooden child.
The unnatural completion of the natural.

iii

How shall the lady say she is not loved
who had all jewels but that single fly? One
of her sons must love her as she is.

Those golden peasants of Heaven by Fra Lippo—
nouveaux riches scrub-drudges of piety—
what can they know of honoring this Lady?

Saints?—Swamp eyes! Is the hound of Heaven a spaniel?
The Lady has infinity in her
eyes. She has till the end of time to look away.

iv

Only the eye that has exhausted time
can look upon the Lady where she is—
a heresy of herself in the natural world

withdrawn forever from the natural world
to the eternal waiting for a world
equal to what she is. She who has suffered

all that nature is—the God who gave her
a God to bear to a makeshift husband. . . . *They'd burn me*
could they hear me pray. But still they know.

v

Only the eye that has exhausted time
can look upon the natural where it is—
between itself and her eternity.

Her light upon the object and the object
within her light: the Lady needs the world
to evidence herself in timelessness

as the world needs the Lady past itself
to be itself excerpted from itself
into the memory she chooses from it.

vi

Let there be adoration by pomegranates:
all that in nature forms unnaturally
the moment of its jewelry in time.

The rescue of perfection from its process
into decay is art and adoration.
The Lady knows no process; she is still

at every instant of her timelessness.
When martyrs send their agonies she sees
only the ruby offered in the wound.

vii

Let there be adoration by pomegranates
in the cauliflower heart of light. Hyacinths for hymnals.
The warts of a cucumber to ravish her fingers.

Is the artichoke no censer? The goddess of fungi
knows the disastrous wood of the sprouting cross
but she has left nature for a serenity.

She will extract from nature what is hers.
And so it is not real, it will adore her:
a natural perfection of the unnatural.

viii

The teeth of a dead dog luminous as phosphor
halted the red-bearded God of ashes
one night outside the city walls. Their light—

pearled in froth and diademed with rot—
delighted the God to poetry in his exile
while all the prose disciples held their breaths

and drew back shuddering from the stench of time.
"In My Father's hand this is another rose,"
the God admonished them. But they were men.

ix

Was there another child for the God to give her?
Was there another child than the God who was
the God who begot him on this infinite Lady?

This is she, selected out of nature
to bear the unnatural child. And he—could he
have stood there with his peasants shrinking from him

had she not made him unnaturally from herself
at a God's bidding: "Be timeless and all times.
Bear me a son to destroy himself from nature."?

x

Let there be adoration by pomegranates
on dishes of terra cotta. Arrangements of seaweed
are the only hair of a God whose halo is oak.

Is there a sceptre more golden than the corn
when her hand is on it? Is there any eye
more than her look out of the lids of seashells?

The Lady who is mother of all bodies
must be wooed with dolls. A mannikin of roots
suckles the breast of Heaven with the child.

xi

Selected out of nature, beyond nature,
the Lady is an infinity of herself
to contemplate her son in all his stages.

Like carp of the air he nuzzles her reverie,
having himself walked out through nature,
beyond nature, to his perpetual pause.

Her hands are mantises in delight upon him.
There is a season of fruits in her nudity.
She lays brocades on autumn in His name.

xii

Let there be adoration by pomegranates
and children dressed in bark—all that in nature
passes through its intricate perfection

arrest in adoration all about her.
Let jugglers and magicians say her masses
and the crystal snakes of Heaven dance for her.

What I have learned to do I give the Lady
instructed by her eye—a glimpse of the world
rumpled upon itself beyond her folds.

And—through the world—her formal beckoning.

On Easter morning two egrets
flew up the Shrewsbury River
between Highlands and Sea Bright

like two white hands
washing one another
in the prime of light.

Oh lemons and bells of light,
rails, rays, waterfalls, ices—
as high as the eye dizzies

into the whirled confetti
and rhinestones of the breaking blue
grain of lit heaven,

the white stroke of the egrets
turned the air—a prayer
and the idea of prayer.

POEMS LOOKING IN

On the Birth of Jeffrey
TO WILLIAM AND BARBARA HARDING

(This is a sort of chorus
  To Jeffrey born in Taurus.
  And to first causes. Ergo,
  To the gleam in Virgo.)

If ever the door close and no wedding
  come to the music; if ever the day
sink down with smoke across it; if ever—and sure—
  the honeyhead grimace and turn away
  from honey, kiss, and bedding—
Jeffrey is your name, and evermore
  William your father and Barbara your mother,
  and who would choose another?

In a country of days, in a war of reason,
  walking on chances, we stop and hear
under the stars of Taurus in the new garden
  at the spring balance of the year—
  Jeffrey, the original voice of season.
At once our three spirea make an Arden,
  and all is possible that starts over.
  Welcome so, Jeffrey, by jonquil and clover,

by the new teeth of the dandelion,
  by the apple tree's white rush, the pink peach,
by scrolls of stars along the bramble walks,
  by the azalea's bursting, and the reach
  of root and shoot from every bush and vine,
by the gloved ladies out to tend their phlox,
  by Burpee's Book and the mail order rose,
  by all that greens the touched earth as it goes—   107

welcome, Jeffrey, welcome to the phylum,
    to the species, to the tribe, the clan,
to the Census Bureau, to the reaching day,
    to the chance and changes of the time of man
    in his garden, jungle, theatre, or Asylum—
and if any man ask "Who is Jeffrey?" say:
    "William is my father, and Barbara my mother,
    and who would choose another?"

Three mountain ranges ranked from drab to blue
Fade backward in the foggy dead of light.
One half-transparent goat in the nearest lot
Kneels tethered to the lawn of appetite,
Grey fur of a grey day on green tables.

El Greco would have known this look of things:
A sky exhaled from hills of smoky stone,
So heavy it must surely come cracking down
The minute prayer relaxes. Bone
Of this world's flesh, animal heat and hunger,

The tethered goat, El Greco in the grass,
Eats his living circle on the scene.
Passion constrained to absolute design.
By ignorance or instinct worlds turn green,
The sky fogs down, and nothing dies of it.

Something of this, a gland's preoccupation,
Keeps the circle going in any look
Of season or weather. See, under the world's smoke
The willow train races along the brook
Puffing green billows, rank and religious spring

Express to goats on road beds sparked with daisies.
The intricate ladings of the dandelion
Fall from its roar. Omnivorous and lean,
He swings his circle on, and from his chin
Dangles the dewy calorie of a flower.

Theology for grey days: I discover
Only stomach is world's absolute lover.

The Size of a Universe

It is a sphere whose circumference is nowhere, whose center is everywhere.
—Variously attributed

The sun is too hot to burn. Burning is a process of oxidation and at the sun's temperature oxygen will not combine.
—From a lecture

If we travel in imagination out into space, taking with us the largest telescope yet made, we lose sight of the earth altogether before we have reached the nearest star. When we have traveled one tenth the diameter of the galactic system we can still see the sun in our telescope, but if we neglect to keep it in view all the time we shall never be able to find it again. It would be like trying to pick out one particular blade of grass in a field.
—F. J. Hargreaves, *The Size of the Universe*

This is the dance of the gases. Do you dream me, Mother?
Fireballs gnaw holes in the dark. Where?
Rivers of nebulae spume the windless ether,
Whirlpool into an eye too hot for burning.

The wounds of a polaroid dogwood bleed
In the tree of space. The angel in the galaxy
Of these blossoms is confused outward, but his tears
Travel only to the center. Which is everywhere.

Quick, think of a world: Novas and novitiates
Of spring spilling the dogwood open, burning
The literal into imagination. A forced landing.
Look through the lens, when? At time, where?

That world—is it yet, my girl in the burning tree?
My father who was a stone at St. Michael's
Shrank to a pebble and I lost him receding
Faster than light through an orchard of pinwheels.

Which way is memory? Not through the deepest lens
Nor by any returning will he be sorted again
From the shales beneath our orchard. At one tenth
The distance nowhere we lost ourselves arriving.

Then *poof!* through stones to pebbles, Father, Father,
The sperm the sperm burns to is another orbit,
The eye the eye stares at is another center.
There's a snail loves me under a backward shale

But I have time-traveled the body of this woman
Against all summons, for where you were
Is an aged woman from whose dark I woke
Screaming your joy in her, her tree's last angel

Receding faster than worlds can be lost from or
Returned to. And *this* is the dance of the gases, my girl of
    lenses—
To be exploded from every gravity.
To be our losses in the hugest eye.

Thoughts on Looking into a Thicket

The name of a fact: at home in that leafy world
chewed on by moths that look like leaves, like bark,
like owls, like death's heads; there, by eating flowers
and stones with eyes, in that zoo of second looks,
there is a spider, *phrynarachne d.*,
to whom a million or a billion years
in the humorless long gut of all the wood
have taught the art of mimicking a bird turd.

"It is on a leaf," writes Crompton, "that she weaves
an irregular round blotch, and, at the bottom,
a separate blob in faithful imitation
of the more liquid portion. She then squats
herself in the center, and (being unevenly marked
in black and white), supplies with her own body
the missing last perfection, *i.e.*, the darker
more solid central portion of the excreta."

Must I defend my prayers? I dream the world
at ease in its long miracle. I ponder the egg,
like a pin head in silk spit, invisibly stored
with the billion years of its learning. Have angels
more art than this? I read the rooty palm
of God for the great scarred Life Line. If you
will be more proper than real, that is your
death. I think life will do anything for a living.

And that hungers are all one. So Forbes reports
that seeing a butterfly once poised on a dropping
he took it to be feasting, but came closer
and saw it was being feasted on. Still fluttering,

it worked its woolen breast for *phrynarachne,*
pumping her full. So once I saw a mantis
eating a grub while being himself eaten
by a copper beetle. So I believe the world

in its own act and accomplishment. I think
what feeds is food. And dream it in mosaic
for a Church of the First Passion: an ochre sea
and a life-line of blue fishes, the tail of each
chained into the mouth behind it. Thus, an emblem
of our indivisible three natures in one:
the food, the feeder, and the condition of being
in the perpetual waver of the sea.

I believe the world to praise it. I believe
the act in its own occurrence. As the dead
are hats and pants in aspic, as the red
bomb of the living heart ticks against time,
as the cyc of all water opens and closes, changing
all that it has looked at—I believe
if there is an inch or the underside of an inch
for a life to grow on, a life will grow there;

if there are kisses, flies will lay their eggs
in the spent sleep of lovers; if there is time,
it will be long enough. And through all time,
the hand that strokes my darling slips to bone
like peeling off a glove; my body eats me
under the nose of God and Father and Mother.
I speak from thickets and from nebulae:
till their damnation feed them, all men starve.

A Sermon Beginning with the Portrait of a Man

The portrait against pine-green and sky: Apollonian
chin nose brow, the eyes reasoned,
the mouth both firm and mobile—you have perhaps
understood this as part of another age;

you will concede at least that there was a time.
Good. A beginning. Assume now
the same portrait against rust wires brick.
Or in someone's apartment. Say, with a drunk behind him.

Is it another man? Had Hamlet
made it to England would he have changed to prose?
Or Sappho to Brooklyn—could she have lived there
truly? Marianne Moore does.

I say you are fools to think it. A house of fools.
Paint him on any surface against whatever
world or wording and hang him anywhere—
there is still this man with the eyes he has earned

quietly, in a contained imagination
neither perfect nor in disorder.
An effort of selection in its process,
he forms an eye to look at the natural world.

SOME SCENES

On Looking East to the Sea with a Sunset Behind Me

i

In a detachment cool as the glint of light
on wet roads through wet spruce, or iced mountains
hailed from the sea in moonfall, or the sea
when one horizon's black and the other burning;

the gulls are kissing time in its own flowing
over the shell-scraped rock—a coming and going
as of glass bees with a bubble of light in each
running errands in and out of the sunset.

Over the road and the spruce wood, over the ice,
and out the picture of my picture window,
the exorbitant separation of nature from nature
wheels, whirls, and dances on itself.

Now damn me for a moral. Over and out,
over and in, the gulls drift up afire,
screaming like hinges in the broken air
of night and day like two smokes on the sea.

And I do nothing. A shadow three feet under
my window in the light, I look at light
in one of the years of my life. This or another.
Or all together. Or simply in this moment.

ii

Lead flags of the sea. Steel furls of the surf.
Day smoke and night smoke. Fire at the smoke's top.
A passion from the world in a calm eye.
A calm of the world in the eye of passion.

The day that sank birdless from staring Calvary
was another. And only another. And no other
than the clucking calm of Eden fussed to rest
from the black bush afire in the first eye.

A calm-in-violence like Aegean time.
Day smoke and night smoke over the palled sea
tensed for a clash of tridents. Far ashore,
a staring army camped beside a temple,

the base of the temple black with powder stains,
the pediment flashing wild in light above.
—A day of the world in which a part of the world
looked at another, two parts of a mist.

At Cassino the dusty German wetting his lips,
his eyes crashed in his face like unhatched birds' eggs
splashed from their nest, looked East from the burning night.
There was no West. Light came from nowhere behind him,

slanted, flowed level, drained. He looked out, waiting.
Where had it come from, the light of his terrible patience?
A dead man waited to die on the shell-scraped
stones of another God, dust of the stones

caked to his body, rivers of blood within him
ran to their dusty sea beside the world.
Calm in his changes, risen from his changes,
he looked his life out at the smoking world.

iii

I have no more to do than what I wait for
under the changing light and the gulls afire
in rays of rose-quartz. Holy ghosts of the sea,

they rise in light from behind me. The light lifts
long from the edge of the world and juts away
over the top of the dark. My life sits

visible to itself, and I sit still
in a company of survivors and the dead.
Jew, Greek, German, man at the edge of himself

in the long light over the worlds he ran to
to save unsaved. I practice the man in all,
clutching the world from the world to praise it.

Landscapes of My Name

> Calling a person by name is recognized as the best method of awakening him when he is sleeping, or of awakening a somnambulist.
> — Freud, *Delusion and Dream*

Like trumpets on a dry mountain, I blow
The high hot note of my name away
Brassy and far on the still Sierras.
John! John! The mountains cry and diminish.

Stone fall would do as well. The silence
Is time past and time to come.
The disturbance of the present sinks like squid
Into the upthrust sea bottoms
Where a different arrangement of a billion years
Suns the fossil by the eagle's nest.
                              John! John!
I cry in the fossil present. My breath, my name,
Wheels once like nesting birds disturbed
From the endless lips of the crevice.
Then settles back into an after-image.

Was there a stir on the mountain? Does God
Believe in me? Did the mountain speak?
Something farther than I could hear blew back my breath.
The mountain and the mountain beyond the mountain.
I see them waver through the seas of time.
An army of my presences
Rang on the shore and the waters divided before me
And a voice woke crying
                              John! John!
From the muddy throat of the gulf.

They were singing Old MacDonald in the schoolbus
With a *peep peep* here and a *peep peep* there after
Margie Littenach had been delivered to the right mailbox
And the gears had gnashed their teeth uphill to the Cliff
  House
Where the driver, shifting gears, honked at the countergirls,
And the tourists turned from panorama all smiles
To remember schooldays, long curls, hooky, and how
The view had always stretched for miles and miles
Where the gentle cumulus puffed small in gentle weather
Putting a cottonfluff roof on the green world leaning down
  hill
To the bluelevelfield of sea, and all together
With an *oink oink* here and a *moo moo* there the children
Were singing Old MacDonald in the schoolbus

When a bolt fell from the compound interest problem,
A rod broke in the third chapter of the Civicsbook
Where the county had no money for inspection in the first place
                    and
Momentum had no brakes, but with a *honk honk* here
And a *honk honk* there went sidewise over tirescreech
Downturning in round air away from panorama where
Even the tourists could tell sea didn't measure each
Stone falling, or button, or bolt, or Caroline Helmhold,
Nor anywhere its multitudinous self incarnadine, but only
  swallowed
What books, belts, lunchpails, pity
Spilled over the touristfaredge of the world and Old Mac-
  Donald

A Visit to Aunt Francesca

Pigment of wax apples bleeds into
The glass refraction of a squint of sun
On marble table tops, and light through wine
Purples our fingers toying with the glass.
It was or never was. At Aunt's command
My hands are poles to orbit colored yarn
Flowing away in little strands of light
From Sunday Fauntelroys and good behaviour
In a dark room divided by the sun.

Three black hairs mustachio her lip
And she was beautiful. The Sèvres cup
Is cracked and glued. I think I hated her.
And that changed too. But still we may not smoke.
Color fades from the daguerreotypes
That manteled all our days. A little more
And all the light is gone. The yarn is gone
In baskets for the night. Only that glimpse—
I cannot reach the rest—a pale gray hand,
A dry kiss like an epigram, a door,
And footsteps sounding on our last goodnights.

March Morning

Black snow, the winter's excrement
On the foul street, thaws
Oil slick puddles traffic-splashed
Back on black snow. Spring
Begins its rumor everywhere,
A new critique and weather.
The ripple is running under
The river's rotting ice,
The winter-lock jaws open.
There is no sun. Only a gray day
Warmer than most.

        Warmer than most,
Colder than some, I mail
Three letters at the corner, turn
On black slush skirting puddles,
Shy from traffic splash, wade
The unclean graves of winter,
Drift-dregs of dead accumulation.
The first corpse is beer bottle green,
A honeycomb of filth on glass.
What's dirty passes. And returns.
What's clean . . .
        What's clean? My dirty death,
My death to walk on, rehearses
Days in a rotting season. Love—
The pulse in a skin glove. Time—
A civic trash on Spring's groundswell. The Scene—
Hellgate at the glacial recession,
Flower faces of children in red hats

Already wanton in water, splashing
Oil-slick puddles on the black snow,
Their mothers scolding from windows.

                           From windows,
You smile, and I,
Having mailed three promises
To the fiction of a world,
Return through these real Limbos
Balancing a bubble of myself
That shines, and is surprised it does not break.

No landsman's eye is ready for this street
    Our wake paves out in glass across the swell,
Yet all souls walk it endlessly out of sight,
    All passengers move astern to breathe farewell
    Farewell farewell and, falling still, farewell
To nothing over nothing under the night.

Then dawn brings up its birds. And standing there—
    Almost as if still standing from the night—
The early riser's raised, yet does not dare
    Accept his change: there is too much in sight
    That is farewell again in every swarming.
There must not be such wings if man is right.

So are we torn who watch our hurtling birds
    Live in the wind, make ramps and chutes of air,
Skim down the trough and shoot the crest. White shards
    Of the over-burning prism broken, their
    Ease with the baited sea makes me half glad
Our death is visible to a spoken word.

Burning and borne on the man-gagging wind
    The searching word performs its dark as far
From any land as God's unquiet mind.
    These do not know their gift but only are
    Their own act of no will. Beware, beware,
The day I die such flies will speck my rind.

One dips until its shadow on the froth
    Touches its wing. Another rides the blow

Motionless upward. West and North and South
    God spills his million company. Below,
    We spill our garbage and the word descends:
On every billow dives an open mouth.

So night again. The gulls drift to the swell
    From gift of air to gift of ocean sleep
And safe at home among our dread, until
    The mouth that opens from the deep
    Swallow all gift into another kind.
No other mouth shall have a tale to tell.

A greensweet breathing
Wakes me from my noon nap
In the high grass by the fence.
Her head swings in above eye level
Weaving through the parade of grasses
Like a Chinese New Year's dragon.

You see a new cow this way:
A sod's-eye view of a munching dinosaur
Peeling the grass from time,
All sweetslobber and greenfleck
In the going going going
Of her machine jaws.

She sees me now,
And roundabout as a steamshovel's boom
Her neck swings its bucket
To the upper air of a question.

But she finds no answer,
Or is used to me and doesn't care,
Or does but forgets,
For back swings the boom
Into the sagebottoms of grass,
And here we are eye to eye
With a single daisy snarled between us
In the stem-tangle
Of sweetdrooling no-time
Going going going
In her machine.

Into the glazed eye
Of the munching cow
Leans the daisy
In a foreground of the hills.

Elegy for Jog

Stiff-dog death, all froth on a bloody chin,
sniffs at the curb. Skinny-man death, his master,
opens the traffic's hedge to let him in.
Jog was his name, silliness his disaster:
he wasn't satisfied to scare the truck,
he had to bite the tire. Fools have no luck.

Domesticity

Because the cat is hungry I must not nap.
Very well. I find a can of cat food
and clamp it into the jaws of the can-opener.
It is one of those hand-crank gadgets on the wall.
I lock the blade in place and spin the crank.
Take that, Marie Antoinette, you mess of fish-heads.

Lines While Walking Home

FROM A PARTY ON CHARLES STREET

Suffer, do you? I think if wounds were art
you'd fill a gallery with scars on plaques,
extractions on red velvet, rare amputations

stuffed and varnished and set out on mirrors
under magenta lights—then throw a party
for Jesus and Mother and Father and all Charles Street.

As for being a beast—you'll have to move outdoors.
Not conscience but the unconscious
stiffens the stallion to the dancing mare.

And one temptation by Hieronymus Bosch
over the radiator won't qualify,
even with Baudelaire propped on the table

between two coupling boys in terra cotta.
Piddle's no rape, rape's no vocabulary,
and Hell's no hobby. One family of Sicilians

has more beasts in to breakfast than you to your nightmares.

Cézanne

When I returned from you in the blue of midnight
I sat by my lamp holding a pear in my hand
and hearing you say: "Tell me again you love me.
Say the words to me. Let me hear the words."

And I could no more understand
the words I said to please you,
than you could have seen that pear, which was also
a word love could ask of me. The pear

was the yellow of a glaze but sanded dull
then lit again by my lamp. These first two lights
where then burned red from below. And up through that,
the black and umber of ripeness freckled it.

And somewhere never placeable in that yellow
a memory of green misted its presence.
I held the pear in my hand and could not tell
where its outline entered the light that made it.

"I will need six colors and all desperation,"
I said to myself, "to bring this pear to truth.
Yet she believes a man may say 'I love you'
on arriving, leaving, and all the night between."

A Shore, Half in a Dream

As if the dawn were dreaming of itself,
I watched the light come gray from sallow shoals
over the metal rocks and the half and half
coil of a small slate surf. A litter of shells
fell from the dream and broke. A plover ran
into the center of the thought. Then,

as if there were a signal in its living,
I saw the dead reach up their shaggy heads
out of the kelp. I saw the kisses leaving
the lips of time like blood that no man heeds.
And the dream said in my head: "I am already
older than my Father in the sea."

As if the sea could be identified
the dead stared at it, and I at the dead,
their eyes like froth, and all their seeing frayed
by unbearable weathers. "Dying is no deed,"
I told the dream. "I pity what we are
in the plover's eye and the soft things of the shore."

And the day dreamed into itself like a melt of skies.
And the night dreamed out of the pines in a loamy mist.
And the dream said: "None but the dead have eyes:
a man sees only what he leaves the most."
I saw the plover run on the stilts of skill,
then bobbin into the air. Across its bill,
like an omega, hung the worm of evil.

FRAGMENTS FROM ITALY

Nona Domenica Garnaro sits in the sun
  on the step of her house in Calabria.
  There are seven men and four women in the village
  who call her *Mama*, and the orange trees
  fountain their blooms down all the hill and valley.
  No one can see more memory from this step

than Nona Domenica. When she folds her hands
  in her lap they fall together
  like two Christs fallen from a driftwood shrine.
  All their weathers are twisted into them.
  There is that art in them that will not be carved
  but can only be waited for. These hands are not

sad nor happy nor tired nor strong. They are simply
  complete. They lie still in her lap
  and she sits waiting quietly in the sun
  for what will happen, as for example, a petal
  may blow down on the wind and lie across
  both of her thumbs, and she look down at it.

One day I went to look at the Mediterranean
and I found myself on an infected hill.
The waves under the sky and the sky over the waves
perfected themselves in endless repetition,
but the hill stumbled and twitched. A desert ate
into its sea front and a gully cankered
its piney back, or what had been
its piney back before that eczema
of stumps and stones and landslides. At its top
like a trollop's hat knocked cockeyed in a brawl
there leaned a tattered strawwork of gray grasses
that fizzed and popped with a plague of grasshoppers.
The grass was salt-burned and seemed wiry enough
to cut the hand that pulled it. And at its roots,
under the leaping gas of the live grasshoppers,
I saw a paste of the dead. There were so many
I thought at first it was the clay-sand soil
from which the wiregrass grew. I could not see
any of the living fall from their leaping
but the dead lay under them, a plague they made
invisibly of themselves who had come to feed
where the grass ate them on an infected hill.

And I saw there was no practice in the sea.

A man-face gathered on the eyes of a child
    measures me from an alleyway. The child
    stirs, but the face has lost its motion:
    the face stares at the traffic and the child
    picks with one finger at a scab on his knee.
    Not looking at it. Not knowing it is there.

He stares at me. I am part of what he knows.
    I am the traffic forever in his eyes
    and damnation, the way all worlds go
    leaving him neither admission nor understanding,
    as, somewhere in a thicket like the mind,
    a gargoyle might stare down at running water.

You would never believe to watch this man
    open his pocket knife to cut his cheese
    (his bread he tears with his hands)
    and lay it down precisely on a leaf
    and tip his bottle off against his mouth
    (which he wipes with the back of his hand)
    and lift the knife again to peel an apple
    so carefully from stem to bud it is all
    one red spiral, and toss it on a bush
    to see it against green and color of loam
    and slap the crumbs from his lap for the birds to have
    before he sleeps with his hat over his eyes
    (for a pillow he joins his hands behind his head)

that all the guns and lances looked to him
    all the maps and marches centered here
    and all the charges climbed this same small hill

that it was always this man in this field
    through all of Europe and the island-South
    the kingdoms and their kings were told about.

What the Roman sun says to the Romans
 (a boy fishing the Tiber with a seine
 while two old men and a tourist watch from the bridge
 that leads to Castel Sant' Angelo, where once
 a cypress forest mourned across the roof
 for a faded emperor gone like his forest
 into the stoneworks)
       what the Roman sun
 (a species of tumulus or burial mound
 as for example pyramids cairns barrows
 and similar monuments common to many cultures)
 says to the Romans (the present structure
 visible on the Tiber being simply the base)
 I have said to you in all the tongues of sleep.

The mountains quiver like a low flame
      on the horizon. They flicker and reappear,
flicker and reappear. Sometimes
there are no mountains and sometimes
they are always there.
                      Mountains
have no need of being seen. They can outwait
all but these repetitions of the air.

Gray Sand, Black Stone, Steel Water, and Figures

She is holding her child in her lap and watching the sea.
The child is gripping a shell with both his hands.
Below her, almost into the curve of the world
a black stick-man stands at the end of rock

and throws his net. Beyond him other stick-men
stand from the shore heaving their arms in the Y
from which the net is slung. The shore is a-toss
from every end of rock. Through surf between

come half-men bearing baskets on their shoulders.
She sits beside the baskets that are brought her.
The silver quivering puddles of the catch
are like a sky reflected up to her,

tipping a-sputter the living parts of water
writhing innumerable light. Beyond, she sees
the gulls like 3's on the air, like 4's on rock.
She sees, or dreams, the great 9 of the whale-spout

rising above the world curve from beyond it.
The pumping houses of light inside their numbers
shine burnished in her eye. Like mother-of-pearl
the heart's valve in the swell, like ruby pipes

the blood-run shimmering on marble bone.
She thinks this terribly of the child. The child
squeals in the tickling air. Light falls like rain.
She holds her child and stares at the silver catch.   *141*

Naples

Hanno vinto le mosche

I saw at a table of the bombed café
a fat man in shirtsleeves,
the stuff of his jersey sweated
to his woman's breasts and belly
so close that the texture of the fat
(like the texture of cottage cheese
or of brains or of boiled cauliflower)
showed through the cloth.

All he had chewed and swallowed
lay ruined in the fat
which pressed at his skin for escape,
a skin strung on a net
of round holes, while through the holes
the fat pressed for escape
held only by the strands of the net
through which, perhaps, his blood ran.

The air was soaked heavy
with the oil-sweet smell of corpses,
that taint which breathes from all
the summer cities of ruin,
their rubble and broken sewerage.
He sat at a table of the bombed café
brushing away the flies that came for him.
Especially for him. There were no others.

He wore his cloud of flies
as a saint wears patience
after his knees have been abused
too long to feel the pain itself.
The flies were his vocation
and he theirs. There can be no
accident in so much meeting:
he was a St. Anthony of flies.

And all of ruined Europe fell about him.
Tiles lay wedged in the gross ruff
at the back of his neck. The dust
of an exploded temple caked
muddy on his bald head and flowed
like half-thickened blood
down and over his eyes,
which were sealed in his fat like navels.

He sat at a table of the bombed café
by the ruined temple, a pediment at his feet,
its writing cracked and crazed. His chair
was a split capital. When he waved his arm
to brush away the flies
a column fell. When he waved it back
another. From every crash the dust
changed into flies and drew a cloud about him.